AF556668
HA HA
For freebies, please visit
funskillbrew.com/freebies
or drop us an email at
hello@funskillbrew.com

Hi, I am SPOOKY, and I am a tooting ghost.
But there's nothing special about it—everyone toots.
Parents toot. Kids toot.
Even my friends toot. Yes, you read that right.

Witches, Zombies, and Vampires pass gas too.

This book will take you on a fun-filled journey of their GROOVY farts.

SCARECROW
AHHH !! Relaxed
BLEEPER!
BLIP!
BOOM!
Ohhh.... NO

THE SCARER EXPLOSION

My farts are giant bombshells with spine-chilling roars that make the birds cover their ears and run from the fields.

Pardon me
MUMMY
SNOOT!
HOOT!
MOOT!

THE BANDAGE RIPPER

As I am all wrapped in layers of linen bandages, my farts have no means to escape. The mustered-up farts are hot, stinky, and steamy. They are the loudest of all farts. They rip off my bandages while escaping, and I need to wrap myself again.

Ready for the GREEN storm?
PIRATE
Aye, Aye !!
BANG!

THE WHOOPING CYCLONE

A whirling vortex of stinky wind, you can see this toot with your own eyes. It spins and spins with a foul breeze that drifts across the sea.

GHOST
HOOT!
TOOT!
POOT!

THE GHASTLY TOOT

My farts are so ghastly that they can haunt houses for generations. They can cause anyone to shutter in fright.

WITCH
AHHHHHH...
BIG relief!
TOOOT!

THE WITCHY TWITCHY SNEAKER

My farts are silent and deadly because they really really stink. No one knows when they come out, and I can easily blame it on the funny-smelling potion.

These farts can cause anyone's nose to twitch.

OOOOPSY !!!

SKELETON

BANG!

THE CRACKING TURBULENCE

I am lanky, but my farts are eerie and robust. They have enough cracking power to wake anybody up at night.

VAMPIRE
BLUH...
BLEH...
BLUH...
TROM!
BROM!

THE TRANCE WAVE

Not just my eyes; even my farts can put anyone in a trance. These farts are so powerful that your brain will freeze, and your jaw will drop.

FRANKIE
PUFF!
BOOF!
TOOOOF!
TUFFF!
TIFFF!

THE FRANKIE BLAST

When my gas has no way to escape, it comes out of my stitched body parts, resulting in a heinous vile fart. These farts cause a sharp stinging sensation to all those who are near.

WAOO!!!
That came
out of my butt
DEVIL
TOOT!
POOT!
HOOOT!

THE DEVIL'S DUNGEON BLOW

This one hovers in the air and delivers the kick to the face. This fart is sneaky and can make you feel trapped inside a stinky dungeon.

ZOMBIE
Ohhh....
SORRY
TOOSH!
BOOSH!
MOOSH!
HOOSH!

THE EARTHQUAKE WHOPPER

My farts multiply rapidly, which can result in a mighty earthquake. This violent shaking can make anyone crumble to the floor in a bumpy motion.

So, you see, everybody farts!
We all do it in our unique way!

Farts are funny and healthy for you. They sometimes can prove to be your superpower too.

If you don't believe me, read my adventures - **How Spooky the Farting Ghost saved Halloween.**

HAPPY HALLOWEEN

Great Food gives Great FARTS;
Great FARTS give Great Smell;
Great Smell gives Great Fear;
Great Fear gives a Great HALLOWEEN;
Great HALLOWEEN leads to Great REVIEWS !!

Make this Halloween Great for us at Funskill Brew,
by leaving us an Honest REVIEW.

More books by Funskill Brew

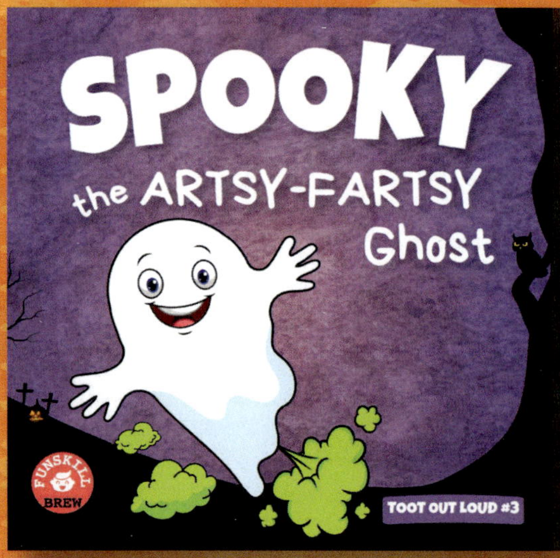

Funny Tongue-twisting Read Aloud Picture Book

Funny Rhyming Story Read Aloud Picture Book